TIM SOUTHEE COLOUR

NEW ZEALAND CRICKETER

MR VIVEK KUMAR PANDEY SHAMBHUNATH

ISBN 979-888546514-4

Short biography of Tim Southee and about life .During writing this book no character & no religious are harmed written by Mr Vivek Kumar Pandey. winner youngest writer award 1st rank in india 2020.He is only one writer can publish 700+ own book that was greatest successfull in his life. This All Credit Goes To My Super Hero Daddy. This book fully colour edition books.

Contents

Foreword

Author biography in English :MY NAME IS VIVEK KUMAR PANDEY . I WAS BORN IN 30 SEP 2002,I AM FROM SURAT GUJARAT INDIA.MY DREAM WAS TO BE GOOD WRITERS ,MY FAMILY SUPPORTED ME TO SUCCESSFUL AND I CAN DO IT MY SELF.How do I write? That is a question, I believe, that can be honestly answered by me."CELEBRATING YOUNGEST WRITER AWARD WINNER IN GUJARAT 1ST RANK" MR PANDEY JI . I may think I did a good job writing something when in reality it could be horrible. The reader is the one who decides the quality of my writing. I do find writing to be natural to me and therefore find it to be a real challenge. My trick as a challenged writer is to do the best I can and know that I am happy with the final outcome. It may take a while to do my best and there may be quite a few problems I run into along the way.

I am not a greedy person those who are thinking about me and my self I never tried it anyone people suffering from sadness ,I trying to get promoted people suffering from happiness and joy in your Life Time. Now in current situation in India and also world people are unemployed and have no many but our indian governor help to people to get free food from ration card , i also take part in leadership team ,i am Motivational speaker , Film script writer. There was my two dream firstly writer and secondly actor & also my own film is upcoming soon i done almost completely completed script for my film .I AM GOING TO SAY WORD OF HEART TOUCH OUT PLEASE READ IT" , firstly i thanks my father he supports me in this field they always getting inspired me by own his words and behavior ,they always said that he was a biggest person in the world in future and also they purchase fruit and chocolate for me in anytime & anyway , firstly my father buy him then call me Vivek you want a chocolate i will say yes papa but how many tell me ,papa: you tell me how much i buy him i told 1 or 2 chocolate but my father purchase whole the boxes of chocolate and they get suprised me. MY FATHER WAS BORN IN " 20 SEPTEMBER" 1971 IN INDIA.

1) MY FATHER FAVORITE CLOTHES IS KURTA PAIJMA AND ALSO STYLES SHOE

2) FAVORITE SINGER IS KISHORE DA

3) FAVORITE STATE GUJARAT AND KOLKATA , HIS VILLAGE IN BIHAR

4) FAVORITE COLOR BLACK AND WHITE

THEY ALSO LOVE cricket like IPL and one day t-20 .they also like watching a News daily and heard the song daily ,they also interested in tik tok video but in current time tik tok is banned in india but also few videos are in you tube. In lockdown time my family and me very enjoy day daily. my father play daily ludo with his sister and son, daughter.they always loved tea and coffee anytime call me "। ववकेि थोडा् चाय बनाओना ववकेि तमु्हारे हाथ का चाय अच्छा लगता है". I make it tea for my father but some reason after the April to june they are suffering from fever and cough , weakness on 6 June 2020 my father death. they not told me say bye bye his life. After death of 6 June on 10 june my mom and dad anniversary.but my father is Best in the world they can do anything for me please take care of father and respect it of your parents.

CHAPTER ONE

Tim Southee Colour

- Tim Southee

1. During writing this book no character & no religious are harmed written by Mr Vivek Kumar Pandey.

Timothy Grant Southee (born 11 December 1988), is a New Zealand international cricketer who plays all forms of the game. He is a right-arm fast-medium bowler and a hard-hitting lower order batsman. The third New Zealand bowler to take 300 Test wickets, he was one of the country's youngest cricketers, debuting at the age of 19 in February 2008. On his Test debut against England he took 5 wickets and made 77 off 40 balls in the second innings. He plays for Northern Districts in the Plunket Shield, Ford Trophy and Super Smash as well as Northland in the Hawke Cup. He was named as New Zealand's captain for the first T20I against West Indies in place of Kane Williamson, who was rested for that game. The Blackcaps won that match by 47 runs.

Southee is known for his ability to generate late outswing at a brisk pace, and later with off cutting slower balls almost like a faster off-spinner on a damp wicket and death bowling. He was the third-highest wicket-taker at the 2011 ICC World Cup (18 wickets at 17.33). He also impressed at the 2015 ICC World Cup, taking 7 wickets in a round robin league match against England.This performance was named Wisden's ODI spell of the decade.

- Early and personal life

Southee was born in Whangarei, New Zealand, and grew up in Northland. He was educated at Whangarei Boys‘ High School and King's

College, Auckland. While at school, he excelled at both cricket and rugby, playing representative rugby for the Auckland Secondary School and Northern Region teams.Southee is married to Brya Fahy. The couple have two daughters.

- International youth representative

Southee played under-19 cricket for New Zealand from 2006 to 2009. His under-19 career included 13 one-day matches – 10 at ICC Under-19 World Cups – and a drawn three-match Youth Test series against India in early 2007. His last youth appearance was at the 2008 ICC Under-19 Cricket World Cup, where he was player of the tournament.

Southee was 17 years old when he debuted in the 2006 ICC Under-19 World Cup on 5 February, against Bangladesh in Colombo, Sri Lanka. He also played against Pakistan, Ireland, the United States and Nepal in that tournament. He ended with 5 wickets at an average of 38.8, and 113 runs at 22.6.New Zealand lost the Plate Final to Nepal.

In 2007, Southee played his only three Youth Tests when New Zealand hosted India. In the second match of the series, which New Zealand won, he took 6–36 and 6–56. He finished the drawn series with 20 wickets at an average of 18.2.

By the time Southee appeared at his second ICC Under-19 World Cup, in Malaysia in 2008, he had already played two full Twenty20 internationals for New Zealand. His bowling saw him named the player of the tournament. He took 5/11 in New Zealand's first match, against Zimbabwe, and went on to take 17 wickets in five matches, averaging only 6.64 and conceding only 2.52 runs an over. Only South Africa's Wayne Parnell took more wickets (18), although he played one more match.] Southee's last under-19 appearance was New Zealand's semi-final loss to eventual champions India, a rain-affected match in which he took 4/29.

Within a month, Southee played in his debut test match. The youth squads he played in included other future internationals Kane Williamson, Martin Guptill, Trent Boult, Corey Anderson, Hamish Rutherford, and Hamish Bennett.

- International career

Southee began his international career as one of the youngest ever to play for New Zealand. He has become a regular member of the international side in all three formats – Twenty20, one-day internationals, and test matches.

- First Twenty20 matches for New Zealand

New Zealand's selectors and coaches took great interest in Southee while he was still playing youth cricket. In 2007 national bowling coach Dayle Hadlee took him to India. Hadlee later said that while there Dennis Lillee had compared Southee's talent to that of Glenn McGrath when he was young. Hadlee, brother of New Zealand Cricket Selection Manager Sir Richard Hadlee, also said that he'd been "whispering in Black Caps coach John Bracewell's ear about the possibility of taking Southee on the upcoming tour of England."

While in the selectors' eye Southee took 6/68 in the first innings of a first class match against Auckland in early December (the innings ended on his 19th birthday). Within a fortnight he was picked to play for a New Zealand XI side in a Twenty20 match against a Bangladesh side on 23 December 2007. The game, played at Northern Districts' home ground of Seddon Park in Hamilton, was a charity match for cyclone relief in Bangladesh, and not a full international. Southee bowled three overs and took 1/31.

- On 30 January 2008, Southee was named in the New Zealand squad for two Twenty20 International games against England. Selection Manager Sir Richard Hadlee said.

"Why delay producing a player of some talent? Perhaps I could compare him with Brendon McCullum when he started – he had a lot of potential. It might take a lot of time for Tim to find his feet but why wait two or three years when someone is in a special category? The feedback we're getting is that this guy has got it."

Southee's international debut took place two years to the day after he'd first played under-19 cricket for New Zealand, on 5 February 2008 in Auckland. He took 1/38. In the second match, Southee was New Zealand's best bowler with figures of 2/22 from four overs.

Most of the New Zealand squad stayed together for the first three one day matches that followed, but Southee rejoined the national Under-19 team for the 2008 Under-19 Cricket World Cup in Malaysia.

- Southee bowling

England were still touring New Zealand when Southee returned home from the 2008 Under-19 World Cup as player of the tournament. The one-day series was over but the three-match test was about to begin. When injury ruled Kyle Mills out of the third Test match, in Napier, Southee was added to the squad and made his Test match debut on 22 March 2008. Aged only 19 years and 102 days, he was New Zealand's seventh-youngest test debutant.

He had an immediate impact in the first day, dismissing Michael Vaughan and Andrew Strauss in his second and third overs, and then later claiming the wicket of Kevin Pietersen. On the second day he took two more wickets and completed a debut five-wicket haul, finishing with 5–55. During New Zealand's second innings, chasing 553, Southee hit New Zealand's fastest half-century in 29 balls. His innings, which ended on 77* from just 40 balls, included nine sixes and four fours.

Only four other Test cricketers had hit more sixes in an innings – Wally Hammond, Nathan Astle, Matthew Hayden and Wasim Akram.

- 2008 season

At the end of the 2007–08 season a survey of New Zealand's first class cricketers named Southee the country's most promising cricketer and in April he was awarded one of New Zealand Cricket's 20 player contracts, placing him among the players with "the greatest likely future value to the Black Caps in the next 12 months".

His rise was reflected in his selection for his first full international tour, to England, Ireland and Scotland from May to July. He played a single test match at Lord's, taking 0/59 in a drawn game, and seven one-day internationals (five against England and one each against the other two hosts). In the ODIs he took 16 wickets, averaging 16.93.

In October New Zealand visited Bangladesh to play three ODIs and two tests. Southee only played the ODIs, taking a combined two wickets for 114. Before the tests captain Daniel Vettori said that there was one position in the team for either Iain O'Brien or Southee. The position went to O'Brien.

- 2008–09 New Zealand season

Southee at a training session in 2009

Through the 2008–09 summer Southee competed for a place in the New Zealand team with more experienced bowlers like Iain O'Brien and Ian Butler. Game-changing performances like the previous summer's five-wicket bags eluded him, though he played 19 matches for his country.

New Zealand's summer began with a short tour to Australia for two test matches. Southee took a combined 5/225 in those matches, going wicketless in the second. Australia won the series easily. Later in the summer New Zealand returned to Australia for five ODIs and a Twenty20 match.

The first inbound tourists of the summer were the West Indies, beginning with a test series for which Southee was dropped. He returned to Northern Districts for the first time since the previous season. The national team picked Southee again for two Twenty20s, across which he took 2/83, and five ODIs (5/180, with two matches being drawn due to rain).

In February 2009 New Zealand visited Australia for a five-match Chappell–Hadlee Trophy ODI series and a single Twenty20. Southee played all the one-day matches but only took three wickets, averaging 84.33. The series was drawn 2–2 and Australia retained the Chappell–Hadlee Trophy. The Twenty20 match, which was a 1-run win to Australia, saw Southee take 1/31.

New Zealand finished the summer hosting India for two Twenty20s, five ODIs and three tests. With Kyle Mills injured Southee played both Twenty20 matches, taking 1/42 and 1/36. New Zealand named a 12-man squad for the first three ODIs with Mills returning alongside Southee and fellow seam bowlers Iain O'Brien and Ian Butler. Initially, Southee and Butler were seen as competing for a starting spot. Butler played all three matches but Southee replaced Iain O'Brien in the third. He was hit for 105 runs without taking a wicketand then dropped from the squad.

Southee played only in the third of the tests, ahead of Mills and Jeetan Patel. India continued to dominate him, and his 30 overs across both innings cost 152 runs for only 3 wickets.The match was a draw, letting India win the series 1–0.Southee wasn't picked to play any full international cricket through the southern winter, which included the 2009 ICC Champions Trophy and 2009 ICC World Twenty20.

- 2009 winter season – lower-level internationals

Southee retained one of New Zealand Cricket's 20 player contracts for the 12 months from 1 August 2009 but through the winter season was left out of Black Caps teams. Instead he played as a New Zealand emerging player, and for New Zealand A. His results were encouraging but Shane Bond's return to international cricket gave him another rival for international selection.

In late July and early August the Australian Institute of Sport hosted a four-team tournament including "emerging players" teams from New Zealand, India and South Africa. The tournament combined both Twenty20 matches (New Zealand played two) and one-day matches (six). Southee played all eight matches for New Zealand, finishing with 12 wickets – twice as many as any of his teammates – at 28.66. He scored runs quickly with 55 off 56 balls in the one-days matches. New Zealand won only one game.

Within a week of the tournament finishing in Australia, Southee arrived in Chennai, India to play four two-day games and a 50-over match with the New Zealand A side. Southee took only three wickets in the two-day matches (one in each of New Zealand's bowling innings, with one game ruined by rain). In the one-day match he took 3/37 off six overs.

- 2009–2010 season

After missing the 2009 winter season Southee became a regular selection for New Zealand in the 2009–10 summer, playing 18 of the season's 22 international matches against Pakistan, Bangladesh and Australia. He also played ten HRV Cup matches for Northern Districts in January.

With bowler Daryl Tuffey unavailable due to a broken hand, Southee regained a place in the New Zealand side that travelled to Abu Dhabi and Dubai to play three ODIs and two Twenty20s against Pakistan.[Before the series captain and stand-in coach Daniel Vettori said he hoped that Southee could "cement his place" in the side. Vettori picked him for all five matches, across which he took seven wickets (four in the ODIs, three in Twenty20s).

The teams moved to New Zealand for a three test series. Before the series Southee played for an invitational XI in a three-day match against the tourists but he "didn't think I bowled very well" and was omitted for the first two tests. He returned to Northern Districts and immediately took 8/27 in a Plunket Shield match against Wellington, the third-best figures in

Northern Districts history. (The Wellington match was marred for Southee by a two-day suspension for swearing.) He was added to the New Zealand team for the third and final test, in Napier, opening the bowling and taking three wickets.

In February Bangladesh visited New Zealand for three ODIs, one Twenty20 and a test. Southee went wicketless in the Twenty20 and first ODI, then missed the second ODI. He returned with three wickets in the third. In the one-off test he opened the bowling and took four wickets across two innings. New Zealand won by 121 runs, giving them a clean sweep of the tour.

Australia's tour included two Twenty20s, five ODIs and two tests. Southee played all of these matches except the first Twenty20. His series began slowly, with only two wickets in his first five games. But in the last ODI he took 4/36 and was man of the match in a 51-run victory (the match was a dead rubber).

Australia won the test series easily. In the first match New Zealand only took five wickets, none of them falling to Southee. In the second New Zealand started by bowling Australia out for 231. Southee had four first-innings wickets and added two more top-order scalps in the second. His two batting scores – 22 not out and 45 respectively – were his best since his debut test.

- 2010 season

Building up to the 2011 World Cup, New Zealand's northern tours in 2010 focused on short forms of cricket. The team played five matches at the 2010 ICC World Twenty20 in the West Indies, a historic two-match Twenty20 series against Sri Lanka in the United States, four ODIs in a Tri-Series with Sri Lanka and India, a five-ODI series in Bangladesh, then five ODIs and three tests in India. The tour to India lasted until December.Southee was a squad member for every series of the season, playing in 14 of these 24 matches.

1. Ten months after missing selection for the 2009 ICC World Twenty20 Southee played the first three of New Zealand's five games in the 2010 edition, taking a single wicket in each, but was dropped on form.New Zealand were knocked out at the "Super 8" stage.

2. New Zealand and Sri Lanka then played two matches at Central Broward Regional Park in Lauderhill, Florida. This was the first time full ICC members played each other in the United States. Across the two games Southee only bowled four overs, ending with a combined 0/25.
3. The three sub-continental countries that New Zealand toured to in 2010 were to host the ICC World Cup in March and April 2011. The tours were seen as important pre-cup practice but New Zealand lost every series. Southee took six wickets in seven ODIs (including four in one match), and four wickets in two tests.
4. In August New Zealand played a triangular one-day tournament hosted by Sri Lanka and including India. They played four matches, all in Dambulla, selecting Southee for the second (a loss to Sri Lanka) and fourth (a "comprehensive thrashing" against India), in which he took four wickets. New Zealand finished third.
5. It wasn't until October that New Zealand toured again, this time to Bangladesh for five ODIs in Dhaka. The tourists were "thoroughly outplayed throughout the series" and didn't win a match. Southee played in two of the matches without taking a wicket.
6. The team to India played three tests (for the first time since March) and five ODIs. New Zealand didn't win a game, though the first two tests were drawn. Southee missed the first test but replaced Jeetan Patel for the last two. He took four wickets at an average of 56. He played in three of the ODIs but didn't bowl in the last of them (India's chase only lasted 22 overs), and took a combined 1/97.

- 2010–11 season: Pakistan in New Zealand

With the 2011 ICC World Cup starting in February, New Zealand only hosted one tour for the summer. Pakistan visited for three Twenty20s, two tests and six ODIs. Southee only missed one ODI, playing all the other matches. He became the third bowler (and second New Zealander) to take a hat-trick in a Twenty20 international, and also took his first ODI five-wicket bag.

The Twenty20 series began on Boxing Day in Auckland, where Southee was named man of the match. He finished the sixth over of the game with a wicket. In his next over he took a hat-trick – only the third in international Twenty20 cricket – giving him four top-order wickets in five balls. He ended with 5/18 in four overs – at the time his best figures in Twenty20 internationals. New Zealand won the match. Southee also took consecutive wickets in the second match, finishing with 2/26. In the third he took 1/53. His bowling average for the series was 12.1.

The first day of the first test saw Pakistan take seven wickets in 65 overs. Southee, batting at 8, played through to the end of the 90-over day with Kane Williamson in a partnership that "prevented Pakistan's complete domination", earning his second test half-century in the process. He was out the next morning for 56, making him joint top-scorer for the innings. Southee also took two first-innings wickets, but over the second and third days Pakistan easily won the match. Established as one of New Zealand's opening bowlers, Southee added two wickets in each innings of the second test. This gave his 6 for the series, averaging 40.5. He also scored another 23 runs in a drawn match. Both his batting and bowling averages for the series were better than his test career averages to date.

- Southee played five of the six ODIs. One was washed out in the third over, effectively making it a five-match series. Pakistan won 3–2. In the first match Southee won another man of the match award for taking his first ODI five-wicket bag, including three in his opening spell. His 5/33 helped bowl Pakistan out for 134, leaving an easy chase for his team.

His figures faded through the series though, and in the last two matches he played (the fourth and sixth of the series) he didn't take any wickets. Across the series he took 7/217, averaging 31.He was awarded the T20 Player of the Year by NZC for the 2010–11 season.

- 2011 ICC Cricket World Cup

Southee was the third-highest wicket-taker at the 2011 World Cup, hosted by India, Sri Lanka and Bangladesh. He was named by the ICC as the 12th man, and only New Zealander, in the "team of the tournament" having finished with 18 wickets at 17.33 (Shahid Afridi and Zaheer Khan jointly topped the wicket-takers). He opened the bowling in seven of New Zealand's eight matches and was first change in the other. New Zealand used 12 bowlers in the tournament, with only Southee and Nathan McCullum bowling in all of their games.

Southee's best figures came in New Zealand's win against eventual semi-finalists Pakistan. He took 3/25, with each dismissed batsman playing in

Pakistan's top five. He took wickets in all of New Zealand's matches, including three each against Kenya, Zimbabwe and Sri Lanka twice – in the group stages and in the first semi-final.

The New Zealand team employed former South African fast bowler Allan Donald as a bowling coach from January 2011. His work was credited as contributing a lot towards Southee's improvement and success at the world cup. Towards the end of the tournament Donald predicted that Southee could be the best swing bowler in world cricket.

The first thing I said to [Tim Southee] when I met him was, 'I want you to take the responsibility of leading this attack. As young as you are, I want you to take that responsibility because you could become the best swing bowler in world cricket in the next year or so' ... I haven't changed his style of bowling, although I think we can improve that. I think he can add the inswinger to right-handers and that's something I need to bring to his game to add some variety.

New Zealand ended the tournament as beaten semi-finalists. He was named as 12th man in the 'Team of the Tournament' for the 2011 World Cup by the ICC.

- Twenty20s in India and England in 2011

Southee had been passed over at the 2011 IPL player auction in January, but shortly after New Zealand were eliminated from the World Cup his form led to the Chennai Super Kings signing him for the IPL's 2011 season, which began on 8 April. The Super Kings coach Stephen Fleming's last test appearance for New Zealand had coincided with Southee's first. In his IPL debut Southee helped the Super Kings to a two-run victory over the Kolkata Knight Riders by conceding only 6 runs in the last over of the match. By playing the IPL Southee gave up the chance to join English county Essex for their domestic summer, but he did join them for the 2011 Friends Life t20 after the IPL. During a victory over Glamorgan, Southee took 6/16 including a hat-trick, establishing the record for best bowling figures for Essex in a t20.

On 26 August 2021, Southee was included in the Kolkata Knight Riders squad for the second phase of the 2021 Indian Premier League (IPL) in the UAE.

- 2011–12 season

New Zealand's season began with a short tour to Zimbabwe which included their first test match since January 2011, ten months before. Southee was injured out of that tour, with his knee not having recovered.Instead his season began with Northern Districts' first class matches, proving his fitness with a haul of 7–37 in the first innings against Wellington.

- 2012 northern season

On the tour to West Indies there were 2 T20Is, 5 ODIs and 2 tests. On a difficult tour NZ won only 1 ODI, losing all the other internationals.

- In the 5-match ODI series Southee was top NZ wicket-taker with 10.

Partnering Neil Wagner and Doug Bracewell, Trent Boult and Southee were called up for the 2nd test at Sabina Park and took 4 and 3 wickets respectively.

The schedule for New Zealand's tour to Sri Lanka included a Twenty20 match (abandoned due to rain), five ODIs (two abandoned, three rain-affected and won by Sri Lanka), and two test matches.

Southee played all three of the ODIs to count, taking only two wickets. In the fourth ODI he picked up three wickets before rain interrupted his over and ultimately led to the match being abandoned.

The test series was drawn one match all – including New Zealand's first win in Sri Lanka in over a decade – and Southee played a major part. He took 12 wickets at an average under 14. ESPNCricinfo rated him the best of the New Zealanders, saying that "on this series' evidence he can be an effective spearhead for New Zealand in the years to come."

- 2012–13 season

By the start of the 2012–13 summer, national captain Brendon McCullum recognised Southee as "our number 1 bowler", an assessment that held even as New Zealand toured South Africa in December and January without Southee, who stayed behind for the birth of his first child and then injured his thumb in a domestic match.

On 14 February Southee returned to cricket after two months. Playing for Northern Districts in the Plunket Shield, he took 1 wickets and scored 3 runs. His form, and Mitchell McCleneghan being ruled out, led to a selection for the squad to play against the touring English team.

Southee returned to the New Zealand test side for the three match series against England. He took only one wicket in the first two matches, but in the third game at Eden Park Southee returned to form, taking 5 wickets as New Zealand fell one wicket short of a series win over the tourists.

- 2013 season

In May 2013, New Zealand travelled to England to play two further test matches. Southee lead the New Zealand attack, bowling superbly to take a career best 10 wickets in the first test at Lord's (becoming the first New Zealander since Dion Nash to do so). He also bowled well in the second test at Headingley, and was widely regarded as unfortunate to finish with just 2 wickets.

- 2014-15 and Cricket World Cup

In the first half of 2014, Southee continued to establish himself as one of the best new ball bowlers in the world, leading New Zealand to a test series victory over a touring Indian side with 11 wickets in a series of consistent performances. He followed this by once again leading the New Zealand bowlers in their tour of the West Indies. Southee again took 11 wickets as New Zealand won their first away series against major opposition in 12 years. By the end of the tour, Southee had risen to number 6 in the ICC world bowling rankings. For his performances in 2014, he was named in the World Test XI by ICC.

In the 2015 Cricket World Cup group match in Wellington, he took his career best bowling figures of 7/33 against England. The opponents were bowled out for 123 and the Black Caps won by 8 wickets with Southee being named Man of the Match.

- 2016–present

Coming at no.10 against India at Dharamshala, Southee scored his first half century in ODIs. This was the fifth highest by any player in ODIs at no. 10 position. After getting dropped in the 1st test versus South Africa for Jeetan Patel he came on as a substitute fielder and caught Hashim Amla.

In May 2018, he was one of twenty players to be awarded a new contract for the 2018–19 season by New Zealand Cricket.

On 3 June 2018, he was selected to play for the Vancouver Knights in the players' draft for the inaugural edition of the Global T20 Canada tournament. In August 2019, in the series against Sri Lanka, Southee became the fourth bowler for New Zealand to take 250 wickets in Test cricket. In August 2019, Southee equaled the tally of sixes by the legend Sachin Tendulkar in test cricket with 69 sixes. On 29 December 2020, in the First Test of the series against Pakistan, Southee became the Third bowler for New Zealand to take 300 wickets in Test cricket.

Southee played his first match in the 2019 Cricket world cup against England on 3 July 2019 at the Riverside Ground. It was his only match played in the entire CWC 2019. In that match, he had bowled 9 overs (54 Balls) giving out 70 runs and taking 1 wicket at an economy of 7.78 in bowling. With the bat, he scored 7*(16) with no boundaries at the strike-rate of 43.75. In August 2021, Southee was named in New Zealand's squad for the 2021 ICC Men's T20 World Cup.

- Captaincy

Southee was named stand-in T20I captain for the first T20I against West Indies. On 29 December 2017, he made his T20I captaincy debut. Under his captaincy, New Zealand won the match. Southee again captained New Zealand for first T20I against Pakistan as Kane Williamson was ruled out due to an injury. New Zealand won the match by 7 wickets.

Southee was named as the captain for the ODI series against England at home due to regular captain Kane Williamson was dropped from the squad due to injury. On 28 February against England, Southee made ODI captaincy debut for New Zealand In April 2019, he was named the vice-captain of New Zealand's squad for the 2019 Cricket World Cup. In August 2019, against Sri Lanka, he was named stand-in T20I captain for New Zealand as regular captain Kane Williamson was rested. In October 2019, Kane Williamson was ruled out of T20I series against England due to a hip injury,with Southee named as captain.

- Playing style

Southee, a right arm medium fast out-swing bowler.While not as quick as fellow new-ball bowler Trent Boult (and the fact that he doesn't keep bowling at 136–141 km/h for long spells in tests), Southee's meticulous accuracy and well disguised variations have allowed him to develop into a genuine spearhead. In 2008 when Southee was first selected in the national team Richard Hadlee remarked of him "He runs in relatively straight, he gets through his action nicely and he moves the ball, particularly away from the batsman". He also established himself as the new opening bowling attack partnership with Boult, having taken 46% of all wickets between them since 2013, especially since the retirement of Chris Martin. In seaming conditions or bowling with an older ball, he tends to bowl more cross-seam deliveries. In damp pitches, he tends to bowl off cutters akin to a fast off spin. In Tests, they are also ably complemented by Neil Wagner's short left-arm seam deliveries.

As a batsman, his aggressive style makes him a useful lower-order batsman. He made his top score of 77* on debut, but since then, his over aggressiveness made him unsuitable as a tailender. He had been dismissed by Nathan Lyon 6 times overall in tests.

CHAPTER TWO

New Zealand national cricket team

- New Zealand national cricket team

The New Zealand national cricket team represents New Zealand in men's international cricket. Named the Black Caps, they played their first Test in 1930 against England in Christchurch, becoming the fifth country to play Test cricket. From 1930 New Zealand had to wait until 1956, more than 26 years, for its first Test victory, against the West Indies at Eden Park in Auckland. They played their first ODI in the 1972–73 season against Pakistan in Christchurch.

The current captain in all formats of the game is Kane Williamson, who replaced Brendon McCullum after the latter's retirement in December 2015. The national team is organised by New Zealand Cricket.

The New Zealand cricket team became known as the Blackcaps in January 1998, after its sponsor at the time, Clear Communications, held a competition to choose a name for the team. This is one of many national team nicknames related to the All Blacks.

- As of 19th November 2021, New Zealand have played 1383 international matches, winning 539, losing 618, tying 15 and drawing 167 matches while 44 matches ended as no result. The team is ranked 1st in Tests, 1st in ODIs and 3rd in T20Is by the ICC. New Zealand have reached two World Cup finals, in 2015 and 2019. They defeated South Africa in the semi final of the 2015 World Cup, which was their first win in the a world cup semi final, but they ultimately lost to Trans-Tasman rivals Australia. In the next World Cup in 2019, New Zealand again reached the final which they lost to the hosts England on boundary count after the match and the subsequent Super Over both ended as ties.

The 2000 ICC KnockOut Trophy win (now referred to as ICC Champions Trophy) stands as one of two ICC tournaments won by the team in their cricketing history. New Zealand also won the inaugural ICC World Test Championship tournament in 2021, beating India by 8 wickets.

- Beginnings of cricket in New Zealand

The reverend Henry Williams provided history with the first report of a game of cricket in New Zealand, when he wrote in his diary in December 1832 about boys in and around Paihia on Horotutu Beach playing cricket. In 1835, Charles Darwin and HMS Beagle called into the Bay of Islands on its epic circumnavigation of the Earth and Darwin witnessed a game of cricket played by freed Māori slaves and the son of a missionary at Waimate North. Darwin in The Voyage of the Beagle wrote.

several young men redeemed by the missionaires from slavery were employed on the farm. In the evening I saw a party of them at cricket.

The first recorded game of cricket in New Zealand took place in Wellington in December 1842. The Wellington Spectator reports a game on 28 December 1842 played by a "Red" team and a "Blue" team from the Wellington Club. The first fully recorded match was reported by the Examiner in Nelson between the Surveyors and Nelson in March 1844.

The first team to tour New Zealand was Parr's all England XI in 1863–64. Between 1864 and 1914, 22 foreign teams toured New Zealand. England sent 6 teams, Australia 15 and one from Fiji.

- First national team

See also: History of cricket in New Zealand from 1890-91 to 1918

On 15–17 February 1894 the first team representing New Zealand played New South Wales at Lancaster Park in Christchurch. New South Wales won by 160 runs. New South Wales returned again in 1895–96 and New Zealand won the solitary game by 142 runs, its first victory. The New Zealand Cricket Council was formed towards the end of 1894.

New Zealand played its first two internationals (not Tests) in 1904–05 against a star-studded Australia team containing such players as Victor

Trumper, Warwick Armstrong and Clem Hill. Rain saved New Zealand from a thrashing in the first match, but not the second, which New Zealand lost by an innings and 358 runs – currently the second largest defeat in New Zealand first-class history.

- Inter-war period

In 1927 NZ toured England. They played 26 first-class matches, mostly against county sides. They won seven matches, including those against Worcestershire, Glamorgan, Somerset and Derbyshire. On the strength of the performances of this tour New Zealand was granted Test status.

In 1929/30 the M.C.C toured NZ and played 4 Tests all of 3 days in duration. New Zealand lost its first Test match but drew the next 3. In the second Test Stewie Dempster and Jackie Mills put on 276 for the first wicket. This is still the highest partnership for New Zealand against England. New Zealand first played South Africa in 1931–32 in a three match series but were unable to secure Test matches against any teams other than England before World War II ended all Test cricket for 7 years. A Test tour by Australia, planned for February and March 1940, was cancelled after the outbreak of the war.

- After World War II

New Zealand's first Test after the war was against Australia in 1945/46. This game was not considered a "Test" at the time but it was granted Test status retrospectively by the International Cricket Council in March 1948. The New Zealand players who appeared in this match probably did not appreciate this move by the ICC as New Zealand were dismissed for 42 and 54. The New Zealand Cricket Council's unwillingness to pay Australian players a decent allowance to tour New Zealand ensured that this was the only Test Australia played against New Zealand between 1929 and 1972.

In 1949 New Zealand sent one of its best ever sides to England. It contained Bert Sutcliffe, Martin Donnelly, John R. Reid and Jack Cowie. However, 3-day Test matches ensured that all 4 Tests were drawn. Many have regarded the 1949 tour of England among New Zealand's best ever touring performances. All four tests were high-scoring despite being draws and Martin Donnelly's 206 at Lord's hailed as one of the finest innings ever seen there. Despite being winless, New Zealand did not lose a test either.

Prior to this, only the legendary 1948 Australian team, led by the great Don Bradman, had achieved this.

New Zealand played its first matches against the West Indies in 1951–52, and Pakistan and India in 1955/56.

In 1954/55 New Zealand recorded the lowest ever innings total, 26 against England. The following season New Zealand achieved its first Test victory. The first 3 Tests of a 4 Test series were won easily by the West Indies but New Zealand won the fourth to notch up its first Test victory. It had taken them 45 matches and 26 years to attain.

9, 10, 12, 13 March 1956
Scorecard

- New Zealand vs West Indies

255 all out (166.5 overs)
John R. Reid 84
Tom Dewdney 5/21 (19.5 overs)
145 all out (78.3 overs)
Hammond Furlonge 64
Harry Cave 4/22 (27.3 overs)
157 all out (80 overs)
Sammy Guillen 41
Denis Atkinson 7/53 (40 overs)
77 all out (45.1 overs)
Everton Weekes 31
Harry Cave 4/21 (13.1 overs)
New Zealand won by 190 runs
Eden Park, Auckland
Umpires: Clyde Harris (NZL) and Terry Pearce (NZL)

- New Zealand won the toss and chose to bat

In the next 20 years New Zealand won only seven more Tests. For most of this period New Zealand lacked a class bowler to lead their attack although they had two excellent batsmen in Bert Sutcliffe and Glenn Turner and a great all-rounder in John R. Reid.

Reid captained New Zealand on a tour to South Africa in 1961–62 where the five test series was drawn 2–2. The victories in the third and fifth tests were the first overseas victories New Zealand achieved. Reid scored 1,915 runs in the tour, setting a record for the most runs scored by a touring batsman of South Africa as a result.

New Zealand won their first test series in their three match 1969/70 tour of Pakistan 1–0.This was the first ever series win by New Zealand after almost 40 years and 30 consecutive winless series.

- 1970 to 2000

Scoreboard - Basin ReserveFebruary 1978. NZ's first win over England

In 1973 Richard Hadlee debuted and the rate at which New Zealand won Tests picked up dramatically. Hadlee was one of the best pace bowlers of his generation, playing 86 Tests for New Zealand, before he retired in 1990. Of the 86 Tests that Hadlee played in New Zealand won 22 and lost 28. In 1977/78 New Zealand won its first Test against England, at the 48th attempt. Hadlee took 10 wickets in the match.

During the 1980s New Zealand also had the services of one of its best ever batsman, Martin Crowe and a number of good players such as John Wright, Bruce Edgar, John F. Reid, Andrew Jones, Geoff Howarth, Jeremy Coney, Ian Smith, John Bracewell, Lance Cairns, Stephen Boock, and Ewen Chatfield, who were capable of playing the occasional match winning performance and consistently making a valuable contribution to a Test match.

The best example of New Zealand's two star players (R. Hadlee and M. Crowe) putting in match winning performances and other players making good contributions is New Zealand versus Australia, 1985 at Brisbane. In Australia's first innings Hadlee took 9–52. In New Zealand's only turn at bat, M Crowe scored 188 and John F. Reid 108. Edgar, Wright, Coney, Jeff Crowe, V. Brown, and Hadlee scored between 17 and 54*. In Australia's second innings, Hadlee took 6–71 and Chatfield 3–75. New Zealand won by an innings and 41 runs.

8–12 November 1985
Scorecard

- Australia vs New Zealand

179 (76.4 overs)
Kepler Wessels 70 (186)

Richard Hadlee 9/52 (23.4 overs)
553/7d (161 overs)
Martin Crowe 188 (328)
Greg Matthews 3/110 (31 overs)
333 (116.5 overs
Allan Border 152* (301)
Richard Hadlee 6/71 (28.5 overs)
New Zealand won by an innings and 41 runs
The Gabba, Brisbane
Umpires: Tony Crafter (Aus) and Dick French (Aus)
Player of the match: Richard Hadlee (NZ)

- New Zealand won the toss and elected to field.

One-day cricket also gave New Zealand a chance to compete more regularly than Test cricket with the better sides in world cricket. In one-day cricket a batsman does not need to score centuries to win games for his side and bowlers do not need to bowl the opposition out. One-day games can be won by one batsman getting a 50, a few others getting 30s, bowlers bowling economically and everyone fielding well. These were requirements New Zealand players could consistently meet and thus developed a good one-day record against all sides.

Perhaps New Zealand's most infamous one-day match was the "under arm" match against Australia at the MCG in 1981. Requiring six runs to tie the match off the final ball, Australian captain Greg Chappell instructed his brother Trevor to "bowl" the ball underarm along the wicket to prevent New Zealand batsman Brian McKechnie from hitting a six. The Australian umpires ruled the move as legal even though to this day many believe it was one of the most unsporting decisions made in cricket.

When New Zealand next played in the tri-series in Australia in 1983, Lance Cairns became a cult hero for his one-day batting. In one match against Australia, he hit six sixes at the MCG, one of the world's largest grounds. Few fans remember that New Zealand lost this game by 149 runs. However, Lance's greatest contribution to New Zealand cricket was his son Chris Cairns.

Chris Cairns made his debut one year before Hadlee retired in 1990. Cairns, one of New Zealand's best all-rounders, led the 1990s bowling attack with Danny Morrison. Stephen Fleming, New Zealand's most prolific scorer, led the batting and the team into the 21st century. Nathan Astle and Craig McMillan also scored plenty of runs for New Zealand, but both retired earlier than expected.

Daniel Vettori made his debut as an 18-year-old in 1997, and when he took over from Fleming as captain in 2007 he was regarded as the best spinning all-rounder in world cricket. On 26 August 2009, Daniel Vettori became the eighth player and second left-arm bowler (after Chaminda Vaas) in history to take 300 wickets and score 3000 test runs, joining the illustrious club. Vettori decided to take an indefinite break from international short form cricket in 2011 but continued to represent New Zealand in Test cricket and returned for the 2015 Cricket World Cup.

On 4 April 1996, New Zealand achieved a unique world record, where the whole team was adjudged Man of the Match for team performance against 4 run victory over the West Indies. This is recorded as the only time where whole team achieved such an award.

- The Black Caps logo.

New Zealand started the new millennium by winning the 2000 ICC KnockOut Trophy in Kenya to claim their first ICC tournament. They started with a 64-run win over Zimbabwe then proceeded to beat Pakistan by 4 wickets in the semi-final. In the final against India, Chris Cairns scored an unbeaten 102 in New Zealand's run chase helping them win the tournament.

- New Zealand won the 2000 ICC Knockout Trophy.

Shane Bond played 17 Tests for NZ between 2001 and 2007 but missed far more through injury. When fit, he added a dimension to the NZ bowling attack that had been missing since Hadlee retired.

- The New Zealand team celebrating a dismissal in 2009

The rise of the financial power of the BCCI had an immense effect on NZ cricket and its players. The BCCI managed to convince other boards not to pick players who had joined the rival Twenty-20 Indian Cricket League. NZ Cricket lost the services of Shane Bond, Lou Vincent, Andre Adams, Hamish Marshall and Daryl Tuffey. The money to be made from Twenty-20 cricket in India may have also induced players, such as Craig McMillan and Scott Styris (from Test cricket) to retire earlier than they would have otherwise. After the demise of the Indian Cricket League Bond and Tuffey again played for New Zealand.

Vettori stood down as Test captain in 2011 leading to star batsman Ross Taylor to take his place. Taylor led New Zealand for a year which included a thrilling win in a low scoring Test match against Australia in Hobart, their first win over Australia since 1993. In 2012/13 Brendon McCullum became captain and new players such as Kane Williamson, Corey Anderson, Doug Bracewell, Trent Boult and Jimmy Neesham emerged as world-class performers. McCullum captained New Zealand to series wins against the West Indies and India in 2013/14 and both Pakistan and Sri Lanka in 2014/15 increasing New Zealand's rankings in both Test and ODI formats. In the series against India McCullum scored 302 at Wellington to become New Zealand's first Test triple centurion.

1. In early 2015 New Zealand made the final of the Cricket World Cup, going through the tournament undefeated until the final, where they lost to Australia by seven wickets.
2. In 2015 the New Zealand national cricket team played under the name of Aotearoa for their first match against Zimbabwe to celebrate te Wiki o te Reo Māori (Māori Language Week).
3. In mid-2015 New Zealand toured England, performing well, drawing the Test series 1–1, and losing the One Day series, 2–3.
4. From October to November 2015, and in February 2016, New Zealand played Australia in two Test Series, in three and two games a piece
5. With a changing of an era in the Australian team, New Zealand was rated as a chance of winning especially in New Zealand. New Zealand lost both series by 2-0

CHAPTER THREE

Let's Know About Cricket

- Cricket

Cricket is a bat-and-ball game played between two teams of eleven players on a field at the centre of which is a 22-yard (20-metre) pitch with a wicket at each end, each comprising two bails balanced on three stumps. The game proceeds when a player on the fielding team, called the bowler, "bowls" (propels) the ball from one end of the pitch towards the wicket at the other end. The batting side's players score runs by striking the bowled ball with a bat and running between the wickets, while the bowling side tries to prevent this by keeping the ball within the field and getting it to either wicket, and dismiss each batter (so they are "out"). Means of dismissal include being bowled, when the ball hits the stumps and dislodges the bails, and by the fielding side either catching a hit ball before it touches the ground, or hitting a wicket with the ball before a batter can cross the crease line in front of the wicket to complete a run. When ten batters have been dismissed, the innings ends and the teams swap roles. The game is adjudicated by two umpires, aided by a third umpire and match referee in international matches.

Forms of cricket range from Twenty20, with each team batting for a single innings of 20 overs and the game generally lasting three hours, to Test matches played over five days. Traditionally cricketers play in all-white kit, but in limited overs cricket they wear club or team colours. In addition to the basic kit, some players wear protective gear to prevent injury caused by the ball, which is a hard, solid spheroid made of compressed leather with a slightly raised sewn seam enclosing a cork core layered with tightly wound string.

The earliest reference to cricket is in South East England in the mid-16th century. It spread globally with the expansion of the British Empire, with the first international matches in the second half of the 19th century. The game's governing body is the International Cricket Council (ICC), which has over 100 members, twelve of which are full members who play Test matches. The game's rules, the Laws of Cricket, are maintained by Marylebone Cricket Club (MCC) in London. The sport is followed primarily in South Asia, Australasia, the United Kingdom, southern Africa and the West Indies.Women's cricket, which is organised and played separately, has also achieved international standard. The most successful side playing international cricket is Australia, which has won seven One Day International trophies, including five World Cups, more than any other country and has been the top-rated Test side more than any other country.

- History of cricket to 1725

A medieval "club ball" game involving an underhand bowl towards a batter. Ball catchers are shown positioning themselves to catch a ball. Detail from the Canticles of Holy Mary, 13th century.

Cricket is one of many games in the "club ball" sphere that basically involve hitting a ball with a hand-held implement; others include baseball (which shares many similarities with cricket, both belonging in the more specific bat-and-ball games category), golf, hockey, tennis, squash, badminton and table tennis. In cricket's case, a key difference is the existence of a solid target structure, the wicket (originally, it is thought, a "wicket gate" through which sheep were herded), that the batter must defend. The cricket historian Harry Altham identified three "groups" of "club ball" games: the "hockey group", in which the ball is driven to and fro between two targets (the goals); the "golf group", in which the ball is driven towards an undefended target (the hole); and the "cricket group", in which "the ball is aimed at a mark (the wicket) and driven away from it".

It is generally believed that cricket originated as a children's game in the south-eastern counties of England, sometime during the medieval period.Although there are claims for prior dates, the earliest definite reference to cricket being played comes from evidence given at a court case in Guildford in January 1597 (Old Style), equating to January 1598 in the modern calendar. The case concerned ownership of a certain plot of land and the court heard the testimony of a 59-year-old coroner, John Derrick, who gave witness that.

Being a scholler in the ffree schoole of Guldeford hee and diverse of his fellows did runne and play there at creckett and other plaies.

Given Derrick's age, it was about half a century earlier when he was at school and so it is certain that cricket was being played c. 1550 by boys in Surrey. The view that it was originally a children's game is reinforced by Randle Cotgrave's 1611 English-French dictionary in which he defined the noun "crosse" as "the crooked staff wherewith boys play at cricket" and the verb form "crosser" as "to play at cricket".

One possible source for the sport's name is the Old English word "cryce" (or "cricc") meaning a crutch or staff. In Samuel Johnson's Dictionary, he derived cricket from "cryce, Saxon, a stick". In Old French, the word "criquet" seems to have meant a kind of club or stick. Given the strong medieval trade connections between south-east England and the County of Flanders when the latter belonged to the Duchy of Burgundy, the name may have been derived from the Middle Dutch (in use in Flanders at the time) "krick"(-e), meaning a stick (crook). Another possible source is the Middle Dutch word "krickstoel", meaning a long low stool used for kneeling in church and which resembled the long low wicket with two stumps used in early cricket. According to Heiner Gillmeister, a European language expert of Bonn University, "cricket" derives from the Middle Dutch phrase for hockey, met de (krik ket)sen (i.e., "with the stick chase"). Gillmeister has suggested that not only the name but also the sport itself may be of Flemish origin.

- Growth of amateur and professional cricket in England

Evolution of the cricket bat. The original "hockey stick" (left) evolved into the straight bat from c. 1760 when pitched delivery bowling began.

Although the main object of the game has always been to score the most runs, the early form of cricket differed from the modern game in certain key technical aspects; the North American variant of cricket known as wicket retained many of these aspects. The ball was bowled underarm by the bowler and along the ground towards a batter armed with a bat that in shape resembled a hockey stick; the batter defended a low, two-stump wicket; and runs were called notches because the scorers recorded them by notching tally sticks.

In 1611, the year Cotgrave's dictionary was published, ecclesiastical court records at Sidlesham in Sussex state that two parishioners, Bartholomew Wyatt and Richard Latter, failed to attend church on Easter Sunday because they were playing cricket. They were fined 12d each and ordered to do penance.This is the earliest mention of adult participation in cricket and it was around the same time that the earliest known organised inter-parish or village match was played – at Chevening, Kent. In 1624, a player called Jasper Vinall died after he was accidentally struck on the head during a match between two parish teams in Sussex.

Cricket remained a low-key local pursuit for much of the 17th century. It is known, through numerous references found in the records of ecclesiastical court cases, to have been proscribed at times by the Puritans before and during the Commonwealth. The problem was nearly always the issue of Sunday play as the Puritans considered cricket to be "profane" if played on the Sabbath, especially if large crowds or gambling were involved.

According to the social historian Derek Birley, there was a "great upsurge of sport after the Restoration" in 1660. Gambling on sport became a problem significant enough for Parliament to pass the 1664 Gambling Act, limiting stakes to £100 which was, in any case, a colossal sum exceeding the annual income of 99% of the population. Along with prizefighting, horse racing and blood sports, cricket was perceived to be a gambling sport.Rich patrons made matches for high stakes, forming teams in which they engaged the first professional players.By the end of the century, cricket had developed into a major sport that was spreading throughout England and was already being taken abroad by English mariners and colonisers – the earliest reference to cricket overseas is dated 1676. A 1697 newspaper report survives of "a great cricket match" played in Sussex "for fifty guineas apiece" – this is the earliest known contest that is generally considered a First Class match.

- The patrons, and other players from the social class known as the "gentry", began to classify themselves as "amateurs" to establish a clear distinction from the professionals, who were invariably members of the working class, even to the point of having separate changing and dining facilities. The gentry, including such high-ranking nobles as the Dukes of Richmond, exerted their honour code of noblesse oblige to claim rights of leadership in any sporting contests they took part in, especially as it was necessary for them to play alongside their "social inferiors" if they were to win their bets. In time, a perception took hold that the typical amateur who played in first-class cricket, until 1962 when amateurism was abolished, was someone with a public school education who had then gone to one of Cambridge or Oxford University – society insisted that such people were "officers and gentlemen" whose destiny was to provide leadership. In a purely financial sense, the cricketing amateur would theoretically claim expenses for playing while his professional counterpart played under contract and was paid a wage or match fee; in practice, many amateurs claimed more than actual expenditure and the derisive term "shamateur" was coined to describe the practice.

- The Young Cricketer, 1768

The game underwent major development in the 18th century to become England’s national sport.Its success was underwritten by the twin necessities of patronage and betting. Cricket was prominent in London as early as 1707 and, in the middle years of the century, large crowds flocked to matches on the Artillery Ground in Finsbury. The single wicket form of the sport attracted huge crowds and wagers to match, its popularity peaking in the 1748 season. Bowling underwent an evolution around 1760 when bowlers began to pitch the ball instead of rolling or skimming it towards the batter. This caused a revolution in bat design because, to deal with the bouncing ball, it was necessary to introduce the modern straight bat in place of the old "hockey stick" shape.

The Hambledon Club was founded in the 1760s and, for the next twenty years until the formation of Marylebone Cricket Club (MCC) and the opening of Lord’s Old Ground in 1787, Hambledon was both the game’s greatest club and its focal point. MCC quickly became the sport’s premier club and the custodian of the Laws of Cricket. New Laws introduced in the latter part of the 18th century included the three stump wicket and leg before wicket (lbw).

The 19th century saw underarm bowling superseded by first roundarm and then overarm bowling. Both developments were controversial.Organisation of the game at county level led to the creation of the county clubs, starting with Sussex in 1839. In December 1889, the eight leading county clubs formed the official County Championship, which began in 1890.

The most famous player of the 19th century was W. G. Grace, who started his long and influential career in 1865. It was especially during the career of Grace that the distinction between amateurs and professionals became blurred by the existence of players like him who were nominally amateur but, in terms of their financial gain, de facto professional. Grace himself was said to have been paid more money for playing cricket than any professional.

The last two decades before the First World War have been called the "Golden Age of cricket". It is a nostalgic name prompted by the collective sense of loss resulting from the war, but the period did produce some great players and memorable matches, especially as organised competition at county and Test level developed.

- Cricket becomes an international sport

In 1844, the first-ever international match took place between the United States and Canada. In 1859, a team of English players went to North America on the first overseas tour. Meanwhile, the British Empire had been instrumental in spreading the game overseas and by the middle of the 19th century it had become well established in Australia, the Caribbean, India, Pakistan, New Zealand, North America and South Africa.

In 1862, an English team made the first tour of Australia. The first Australian team to travel overseas consisted of Aboriginal stockmen who toured England in 1868. The first One Day International match was played on 5 January 1971 between Australia and England at the Melbourne Cricket Ground.

In 1876–77, an England team took part in what was retrospectively recognised as the first-ever Test match at the Melbourne Cricket Ground against Australia. The rivalry between England and Australia gave birth to The Ashes in 1882, and this has remained Test cricket's most famous contest. Test cricket began to expand in 1888–89 when South Africa played England.

- World cricket in the 20th century

The inter-war years were dominated by Australia's Don Bradman, statistically the greatest Test batter of all time. Test cricket continued to expand during the 20th century with the addition of the West Indies (1928),

New Zealand (1930) and India (1932) before the Second World War and then Pakistan (1952), Sri Lanka (1982), Zimbabwe (1992), Bangladesh (2000), Ireland and Afghanistan (both 2018) in the post-war period. South Africa was banned from international cricket from 1970 to 1992 as part of the apartheid boycott.

- The rise of limited overs cricket

Cricket entered a new era in 1963 when English counties introduced the limited overs variant. As it was sure to produce a result, limited overs cricket was lucrative and the number of matches increased. The first Limited Overs International was played in 1971 and the governing International Cricket Council (ICC), seeing its potential, staged the first limited overs Cricket World Cup in 1975. In the 21st century, a new limited overs form, Twenty20, made an immediate impact. On 22 June 2017, Afghanistan and Ireland became the 11th and 12th ICC full members, enabling them to play Test cricket.

- A typical cricket field.

In cricket, the rules of the game are specified in a code called The Laws of Cricket (hereinafter called "the Laws") which has a global remit. There are 42 Laws (always written with a capital "L"). The earliest known version of the code was drafted in 1744 and, since 1788, it has been owned and maintained by its custodian, the Marylebone Cricket Club (MCC) in London.

- Playing area

Cricket is a bat-and-ball game played on a cricket field between two teams of eleven players each. The field is usually circular or oval in shape and the edge of the playing area is marked by a boundary, which may be a fence, part of the stands, a rope, a painted line or a combination of these; the boundary must if possible be marked along its entire length.

In the approximate centre of the field is a rectangular pitch (see image, below) on which a wooden target called a wicket is sited at each end; the wickets are placed 22 yards (20 m) apart. The pitch is a flat surface 10 feet (3.0 m) wide, with very short grass that tends to be worn away as the game progresses (cricket can also be played on artificial surfaces, notably matting). Each wicket is made of three wooden stumps topped by two bails.

- Cricket pitch and creases

As illustrated above, the pitch is marked at each end with four white painted lines: a bowling crease, a popping crease and two return creases. The three stumps are aligned centrally on the bowling crease, which is eight feet eight inches long. The popping crease is drawn four feet in front of the bowling crease and parallel to it; although it is drawn as a twelve-foot line (six feet either side of the wicket), it is, in fact, unlimited in length. The return creases are drawn at right angles to the popping crease so that they intersect the ends of the bowling crease; each return crease is drawn as an eight-foot line, so that it extends four feet behind the bowling crease, but is also, in fact, unlimited in length.

Before a match begins, the team captains (who are also players) toss a coin to decide which team will bat first and so take the first innings. Innings is the term used for each phase of play in the match.In each innings, one team bats, attempting to score runs, while the other team bowls and fields the ball, attempting to restrict the scoring and dismiss the batters. When the first innings ends, the teams change roles; there can be two to four innings depending upon the type of match. A match with four scheduled innings is played over three to five days; a match with two scheduled innings is usually completed in a single day. During an innings, all eleven members of the fielding team take the field, but usually only two members of the batting team are on the field at any given time. The exception to this is if a batter has any type of illness or injury restricting his or her ability to run, in this case the batter is allowed a runner who can run between the wickets when the batter hits a scoring run or runs,though this does not apply in international cricket. The order of batters is usually announced just before the match, but it can be varied.

The main objective of each team is to score more runs than their opponents but, in some forms of cricket, it is also necessary to dismiss all of the opposition batters in their final innings in order to win the match, which would otherwise be drawn. If the team batting last is all out having scored fewer runs than their opponents, they are said to have "lost by n runs" (where n is the difference between the aggregate number of runs scored by the teams). If the team that bats last scores enough runs to win, it is said to have "won by n wickets", where n is the number of wickets left to fall. For example, a team that passes its opponents‘ total having lost six wickets (i.e., six of their batters have been dismissed) have won the match "by four wickets".

In a two-innings-a-side match, one team's combined first and second innings total may be less than the other side's first innings total. The team with the greater score is then said to have "won by an innings and n runs", and does not need to bat again: n is the difference between the two teams' aggregate scores. If the team batting last is all out, and both sides have scored the same number of runs, then the match is a tie; this result is quite rare in matches of two innings a side with only 62 happening in first-class matches from the earliest known instance in 1741 until January 2017. In the traditional form of the game, if the time allotted for the match expires before either side can win, then the game is declared a draw.

If the match has only a single innings per side, then a maximum number of overs applies to each innings. Such a match is called a "limited overs" or "one-day" match, and the side scoring more runs wins regardless of the number of wickets lost, so that a draw cannot occur. In some cases, ties are broken by having each team bat for a one-over innings known as a Super Over; subsequent Super Overs may be played if the first Super Over ends in a tie. If this kind of match is temporarily interrupted by bad weather, then a complex mathematical formula, known as the Duckworth–Lewis–Stern method after its developers, is often used to recalculate a new target score. A one-day match can also be declared a "no-result" if fewer than a previously agreed number of overs have been bowled by either team, in circumstances that make normal resumption of play impossible; for example, wet weather.

In all forms of cricket, the umpires can abandon the match if bad light or rain makes it impossible to continue. There have been instances of entire matches, even Test matches scheduled to be played over five days, being lost to bad weather without a ball being bowled: for example, the third Test of the 1970/71 series in Australia.

- Innings

The innings (ending with 's' in both singular and plural form) is the term used for each phase of play during a match. Depending on the type of match being played, each team has either one or two innings. Sometimes all eleven members of the batting side take a turn to bat but, for various reasons, an innings can end before they have all done so. The innings terminates if the batting team is "all out", a term defined by the Laws: "at the fall of a wicket or the retirement of a batter, further balls remain to be bowled but no further batter is available to come in". In this situation, one of the batters has not been dismissed and is termed not out; this is because he has no partners left and there must always be two active batters while the innings is in progress.

- An innings may end early while there are still two not out batters

the batting team's captain may declare the innings closed even though some of his players have not had a turn to bat: this is a tactical decision by the captain, usually because he believes his team have scored sufficient runs and need time to dismiss the opposition in their innings

the set number of overs (i.e., in a limited overs match) have been bowled

the match has ended prematurely due to bad weather or running out of time

in the final innings of the match, the batting side has reached its target and won the game.

- Overs

The Laws state that, throughout an innings, "the ball shall be bowled from each end alternately in overs of 6 balls". The name "over" came about because the umpire calls "Over!" when six balls have been bowled. At this point, another bowler is deployed at the other end, and the fielding side changes ends while the batters do not. A bowler cannot bowl two successive overs, although a bowler can (and usually does) bowl alternate overs, from the same end, for several overs which are termed a "spell". The batters do not change ends at the end of the over, and so the one who was non-striker is now the striker and vice versa. The umpires also change positions so that the one who was at "square leg" now stands behind the wicket at the non-striker's end and vice versa.

- Clothing and equipment

English cricketer W. G. Grace "taking guard" in 1883. His pads and bat are very similar to those used today. The gloves have evolved somewhat. Many modern players use more defensive equipment than were available to Grace, most notably helmets and arm guards.

The wicket-keeper (a specialised fielder behind the batter) and the batters wear protective gear because of the hardness of the ball, which can be delivered at speeds of more than 145 kilometres per hour (90 mph) and presents a major health and safety concern. Protective clothing includes pads (designed to protect the knees and shins), batting gloves or wicket-keeper's gloves for the hands, a safety helmet for the head and a box for male players inside the trousers (to protect the crotch area). Some batters wear additional padding inside their shirts and trousers such as thigh pads, arm pads, rib protectors and shoulder pads. The only fielders allowed to wear protective gear are those in positions very close to the batter (i.e., if they are alongside or in front of him), but they cannot wear gloves or external leg guards.

Subject to certain variations, on-field clothing generally includes a collared shirt with short or long sleeves; long trousers; woolen pullover (if needed); cricket cap (for fielding) or a safety helmet; and spiked shoes or boots to increase traction. The kit is traditionally all white and this remains the case in Test and first-class cricket but, in limited overs cricket, team colours are worn instead.

- Bat and ball

Two types of cricket ball, both of the same size:

i) A used white ball. White balls are mainly used in limited overs cricket, especially in matches played at night, under floodlights (left).

ii) A used red ball. Red balls are used in Test cricket, first-class cricket and some other forms of cricket (right).

The essence of the sport is that a bowler delivers (i.e., bowls) the ball from his or her end of the pitch towards the batter who, armed with a bat, is "on strike" at the other end (see next sub-section: Basic gameplay).

The bat is made of wood, usually Salix alba (white willow), and has the shape of a blade topped by a cylindrical handle. The blade must not be more than 4.25 inches (10.8 cm) wide and the total length of the bat not more than 38 inches (97 cm). There is no standard for the weight, which is usually between 2 lb 7 oz and 3 lb (1.1 and 1.4 kg).

The ball is a hard leather-seamed spheroid, with a circumference of 9 inches (23 cm). The ball has a "seam": six rows of stitches attaching the leather shell of the ball to the string and cork interior. The seam on a new ball is prominent and helps the bowler propel it in a less predictable manner. During matches, the quality of the ball deteriorates to a point where it is no longer usable; during the course of this deterioration, its behaviour in flight will change and can influence the outcome of the match. Players will, therefore, attempt to modify the ball's behaviour by modifying its physical properties. Polishing the ball and wetting it with sweat or saliva is legal, even when the polishing is deliberately done on one side only to increase the ball's swing through the air, but the acts of rubbing other substances into the ball, scratching the surface or picking at the seam are illegal ball tampering.

- Player roles

Basic gameplay: bowler to batter

During normal play, thirteen players and two umpires are on the field. Two of the players are batters and the rest are all eleven members of the fielding team. The other nine players in the batting team are off the field in the pavilion. The image with overlay below shows what is happening when a ball is being bowled and which of the personnel are on or close to the pitch.

- Return crease

In the photo, the two batters (3 & 8; wearing yellow) have taken position at each end of the pitch (6). Three members of the fielding team (4, 10 & 11; wearing dark blue) are in shot. One of the two umpires (1; wearing white hat) is stationed behind the wicket (2) at the bowler's (4) end of the pitch. The bowler (4) is bowling the ball (5) from his end of the pitch to the batter at the other end who is called the "striker". The other batter (3) at the bowling end is called the "non-striker". The wicket-keeper (10), who is a specialist, is positioned behind the striker's wicket (9) and behind him stands one of the fielders in a position called "first slip" (11). While the bowler and the first slip are wearing conventional kit only, the two batters and the wicket-keeper are wearing protective gear including safety helmets, padded gloves and leg guards (pads).

While the umpire (1) in shot stands at the bowler's end of the pitch, his colleague stands in the outfield, usually in or near the fielding position called "square leg", so that he is in line with the popping crease (7) at the striker's end of the pitch. The bowling crease (not numbered) is the one on which the wicket is located between the return creases (12). The bowler (4) intends to hit the wicket (9) with the ball (5) or, at least, to prevent the striker (8) from scoring runs. The striker (8) intends, by using his bat, to defend his wicket and, if possible, to hit the ball away from the pitch in order to score runs.

Some players are skilled in both batting and bowling, or as either or these as well as wicket-keeping, so are termed all-rounders. Bowlers are classified according to their style, generally as fast bowlers, seam bowlers or spinners. Batters are classified according to whether they are right-handed or left-handed.

- Fielding

Of the eleven fielders, three are in shot in the image above. The other eight are elsewhere on the field, their positions determined on a tactical basis by the captain or the bowler. Fielders often change position between deliveries, again as directed by the captain or bowler.

If a fielder is injured or becomes ill during a match, a substitute is allowed to field instead of him, but the substitute cannot bowl or act as a captain, except in the case of concussion substitutes in international cricket. The substitute leaves the field when the injured player is fit to return. The Laws of Cricket were updated in 2017 to allow substitutes to act as wicket-keepers.

- Bowling and dismissal

Glenn McGrath of Australia holds the world record for most wickets in the Cricket World Cup.

Most bowlers are considered specialists in that they are selected for the team because of their skill as a bowler, although some are all-rounders and even specialist batters bowl occasionally. The specialists bowl several times during an innings but may not bowl two overs consecutively. If the captain wants a bowler to "change ends", another bowler must temporarily fill in so that the change is not immediate.

A bowler reaches his delivery stride by means of a "run-up" and an over is deemed to have begun when the bowler starts his run-up for the first delivery of that over, the ball then being "in play".

Fast bowlers, needing momentum, take a lengthy run up while bowlers with a slow delivery take no more than a couple of steps before bowling. The fastest bowlers can deliver the ball at a speed of over 145 kilometres per hour (90 mph) and they sometimes rely on sheer speed to try to defeat the batter, who is forced to react very quickly.

Other fast bowlers rely on a mixture of speed and guile by making the ball seam or swing (i.e. curve) in flight. This type of delivery can deceive a batter into miscuing his shot, for example, so that the ball just touches the edge of the bat and can then be "caught behind" by the wicket-keeper or a slip fielder. At the other end of the bowling scale is the spin bowler who bowls at a relatively slow pace and relies entirely on guile to deceive the batter. A spinner will often "buy his wicket" by "tossing one up" (in a slower, steeper parabolic path) to lure the batter into making a poor shot. The batter has to be very wary of such deliveries as they are often "flighted" or spun so that the ball will not behave quite as he expects and he could be "trapped" into getting himself out. In between the pacemen and the spinners are the medium paced seamers who rely on persistent accuracy to try to contain the rate of scoring and wear down the batter's concentration.

There are nine ways in which a batter can be dismissed: five relatively common and four extremely rare. The common forms of dismissal are bowled, caught, leg before wicket (lbw), run out and stumped. Rare methods are hit wicket,hit the ball twice, obstructing the field and timed out. The Laws state that the fielding team, usually the bowler in practice, must appeal for a dismissal before the umpire can give his decision. If the batter is out, the umpire raises a forefinger and says "Out!"; otherwise, he will shake his head and say "Not out".There is, effectively, a tenth method of dismissal, retired out, which is not an on-field dismissal as such but rather a retrospective one for which no fielder is credited.

- Batting, runs and extras

The directions in which a right-handed batter, facing down the page, intends to send the ball when playing various cricketing shots. The diagram for a left-handed batter is a mirror image of this one.

Batters take turns to bat via a batting order which is decided beforehand by the team captain and presented to the umpires, though the order remains flexible when the captain officially nominates the team. Substitute batters are generally not allowed, except in the case of concussion substitutes in international cricket.

In order to begin batting the batter first adopts a batting stance. Standardly, this involves adopting a slight crouch with the feet pointing across the front of the wicket, looking in the direction of the bowler, and holding the bat so it passes over the feet and so its tip can rest on the ground near to the toes of the back foot.

A skilled batter can use a wide array of "shots" or "strokes" in both defensive and attacking mode. The idea is to hit the ball to the best effect with the flat surface of the bat's blade. If the ball touches the side of the bat it is called an "edge". The batter does not have to play a shot and can allow the ball to go through to the wicketkeeper. Equally, he does not have to attempt a run when he hits the ball with his bat. Batters do not always seek to hit the ball as hard as possible, and a good player can score runs just by making a deft stroke with a turn of the wrists or by simply "blocking" the ball but directing it away from fielders so that he has time to take a run. A wide variety of shots are played, the batter's repertoire including strokes named according to the style of swing and the direction aimed: e.g., "cut", "drive", "hook", "pull".

The batter on strike (i.e. the "striker") must prevent the ball hitting the wicket, and try to score runs by hitting the ball with his bat so that he and his partner have time to run from one end of the pitch to the other before the fielding side can return the ball. To register a run, both runners must touch the ground behind the popping crease with either their bats or their bodies (the batters carry their bats as they run). Each completed run increments the score of both the team and the striker.

- Sachin Tendulkar is the only player to have scored one hundred international centuries

The decision to attempt a run is ideally made by the batter who has the better view of the ball's progress, and this is communicated by calling: usually "yes", "no" or "wait". More than one run can be scored from a single hit: hits worth one to three runs are common, but the size of the field is such that it is usually difficult to run four or more. To compensate for this, hits that reach the boundary of the field are automatically awarded four runs if the ball touches the ground en route to the boundary or six runs if the ball clears the boundary without touching the ground within the boundary. In these cases the batters do not need to run. Hits for five are unusual and generally rely on the help of "overthrows" by a fielder returning the ball. If an odd number of runs is scored by the striker, the two batters have changed ends, and the one who was non-striker is now the striker. Only the striker can score individual runs, but all runs are added to the team's total.

Additional runs can be gained by the batting team as extras (called "sundries" in Australia) due to errors made by the fielding side. This is achieved in four ways: no-ball, a penalty of one extra conceded by the bowler if he breaks the rules; wide, a penalty of one extra conceded by the bowler if he bowls so that the ball is out of the batter's reach bye, an extra awarded if the batter misses the ball and it goes past the wicket-keeper and gives the batters time to run in the conventional way leg bye, as for a bye except that the ball has hit the batter's body, though not his bat. If the bowler has conceded a no-ball or a wide, his team incurs an additional penalty because that ball (i.e., delivery) has to be bowled again and hence the batting side has the opportunity to score more runs from this extra ball.

- Specialist roles

Captain (cricket) and Wicket-keeper

The captain is often the most experienced player in the team, certainly the most tactically astute, and can possess any of the main skillsets as a batter, a bowler or a wicket-keeper. Within the Laws, the captain has certain responsibilities in terms of nominating his players to the umpires before the match and ensuring that his players conduct themselves "within the spirit and traditions of the game as well as within the Laws".

The wicket-keeper (sometimes called simply the "keeper") is a specialist fielder subject to various rules within the Laws about his equipment and demeanour. He is the only member of the fielding side who can effect a stumping and is the only one permitted to wear gloves and external leg guards. Depending on their primary skills, the other ten players in the team tend to be classified as specialist batters or specialist bowlers. Generally, a team will include five or six specialist batters and four or five specialist bowlers, plus the wicket-keeper.

- Umpires and scorers

Umpire (cricket), Scoring (cricket), and Cricket statistics

An umpire signals a decision to the scorers

The game on the field is regulated by the two umpires, one of whom stands behind the wicket at the bowler's end, the other in a position called "square leg" which is about 15–20 metres away from the batter on strike and in line with the popping crease on which he is taking guard. The umpires have several responsibilities including adjudication on whether a ball has been correctly bowled (i.e., not a no-ball or a wide); when a run is scored; whether a batter is out (the fielding side must first appeal to the umpire, usually with the phrase "How's that?" or "Owzat?"); when intervals start and end; and the suitability of the pitch, field and weather for playing the game. The umpires are authorised to interrupt or even abandon a match due to circumstances likely to endanger the players, such as a damp pitch or deterioration of the light.

Off the field in televised matches, there is usually a third umpire who can make decisions on certain incidents with the aid of video evidence. The third umpire is mandatory under the playing conditions for Test and Limited Overs International matches played between two ICC full member countries. These matches also have a match referee whose job is to ensure that play is within the Laws and the spirit of the game.

The match details, including runs and dismissals, are recorded by two official scorers, one representing each team. The scorers are directed by the hand signals of an umpire . For example, the umpire raises a forefinger to signal that the batter is out (has been dismissed); he raises both arms above his head if the batter has hit the ball for six runs. The scorers are required by the Laws to record all runs scored, wickets taken and overs bowled; in practice, they also note significant amounts of additional data relating to the game.

A match's statistics are summarised on a scorecard. Prior to the popularisation of scorecards, most scoring was done by men sitting on vantage points cuttings notches on tally sticks and runs were originally called notches.According to Rowland Bowen, the earliest known scorecard templates were introduced in 1776 by T. Pratt of Sevenoaks and soon came into general use.It is believed that scorecards were printed and sold at Lord's for the first time in 1846.

- thank you for buy & read this book

  have a great day of your
  from : Mr Vivek Kumar Pandey

- This All Credit Goes To My Super Hero Daddy. Always Love You dad

Printed by Libri Plureos GmbH in Hamburg,
Germany